BLUE

HBJ —Nova✳Edition—
SCIENCE

Elizabeth K. Cooper
formerly Coordinator
of Teacher Training
University of California

Paul E. Blackwood
formerly Specialist for
Science Education
U.S. Office of Education

John A. Boeschen
formerly Science Teacher
Pinole, California

Morsley G. Giddings
Professor of Education
Brooklyn College, City University
of New York

Arthur A. Carin
Professor of Elementary and
Early Childhood Education and
Director of Environmental Education
Queens College
City University of New York

Biology and Ecology
Garrett Hardin
Emeritus Professor of
Human Ecology
University of California
Santa Barbara, California

Cooperative Learning
David W. Johnson
Professor of Educational
Psychology
College of Education
University of Minnesota
Minneapolis, Minnesota

Roger T. Johnson
Professor of Curriculum
and Instruction
College of Education
University of Minnesota
Minneapolis, Minnesota

Biology and Genetics
Richard C. Lewontin
Professor, Harvard University
Cambridge, Massachusetts

Geology and Earth Science
Alistair W. McCrone
Professor of Geology
Humboldt State University
Arcata, California

Physics
Franklin Miller, Jr.
Emeritus Professor of Physics
Kenyon College
Gambier, Ohio

Astronomy and Science Education
Fletcher G. Watson
Emeritus Professor
Harvard University
Cambridge, Massachusetts

Advisory Board

Judy H. Dennison
Coordinator of
Elementary Science
Fulton County Schools
Atlanta, Georgia

Kathleen Donnellan
Elementary Science
Resource Teacher
Springfield Public Schools
Springfield, Massachusetts

Iris Maney
Title II Staff
Development Specialist
Orleans Parish
New Orleans, Louisiana

Dale Rose
Supervisor of Science
Hampton School
Administration Center
Hampton, Virginia

LaWanna S. White
Science Supervisor
Cleveland Public Schools
Cleveland, Ohio

HBJ **HARCOURT BRACE JOVANOVICH, PUBLISHERS**
Orlando   San Diego   Chicago   Dallas

Reviewers

Frances M. Culpepper
Science Coordinator, K-12
Instructional Services Center
Atlanta, Georgia

Robert W. Deem
Former Coordinator of Science,
    Health and Outdoor Education
School District 446
Elgin, Illinois

Marjorie Slavick Frank
Adjunct Faculty
School of Education
Manhattan College
Bronx, New York

Sister Anna Marie Goetz, R.S.M.
St. Maurice School
Pittsburgh, Pennsylvania

Deborah G. Gozzard
Science Teacher
Lynnhaven Junior High School
Virginia Beach, Virginia

Darlene Harmon
Clausell Elementary School
Jackson, Mississippi

Ernestine Hightower
Whittier Elementary School
Lawton, Oklahoma

Janet Iona
Adams County School District #12
Northglenn, Colorado

Patricia C. Manning
Professor, College of Education
University of Central Florida
Orlando, Florida

Thomasena Woods
Science Supervisor
Newport News Public Schools
Newport News, Virginia

PRINTED IN THE UNITED STATES OF AMERICA

ISBN 0-15-364321-8

PICTURE CREDITS

Key: (t) top, (b) bottom, (l) left, (r) right, (c) center.

COVER: Zig Leszczynski/Animals Animals.

Contents Pages: iii(t), Jim Cartier/Photo Researchers, (ct) Bruce A. MacDonald/Earth Scenes, (c) William Calvert/E. R. Degginger, (cb) B. Kreye/Image Bank, (b) E. R. Degginger; **iv**(t), L. L. T. Rhodes/Taurus, (ct), Steve Wilson/Entheos, (c) J. Alex Langley/DPI, (cb) Ann Hagen Griffiths/Omni Photo Communications, (b) Phil Degginger.

ILLUSTRATORS: Philip M. Veloric, Publisher's Graphics, Artists International, Mulvey Associates, Ex Libris.

UNIT 1: Pages; **vi**(l), Lawrence Migdale/Photo Researchers, (tr) Eric Hausserman/Photo Researchers, (br) Jim Cartier/Photo Researchers; **1**(t), Susan McCartney/Photo Researchers, (bl) Omni-Photo Communications, (br) Robert Knowles/Photo Researchers; **2**(tl), Cary Wolinsky/Stock, Boston, (tr) Ann Hagen Griffiths/Omni-Photo Communications, (bl) Erika Stone/Peter Arnold, (br) Pam Hasegawa/Taurus; **3**(tl), Whitney L. Lane/Image Bank, (tr) Richard Hutchings/Photo Researchers, (bl) HBJ, (br) B. Kreye/Image Bank; **4**(tl), Focus On Sports, (tr) Bruce Roberts/Photo Researchers, (cr) Richard Hutchings/Photo Researchers, (br) HBJ; **5**, HBJ; **6**(tl), Peter Southwick/Stock, Boston, (tr, cl, br), HBJ, (bl) Kenneth Karp; **7**(tl), Pam Hasegawa/Taurus, (br) Elaine Wicks/O. S. R./Taurus; **8-9**, HBJ;

UNIT 2: 14(l), E. R. Degginger, (tr, br) HBJ; **15**(t), HBJ, (bl) Patrick Grace/Photo Researchers, (br) Milton Heiberg/Photo Researchers; **16**(tl), E. R. Degginger, (tr, bl) Grant Heilman, (cr) Manuel Rodriguez, (br) Alan Pitcairn/Grant Heilman; **17**(tl), Bruce A. McDonald/Earth Scenes, (tr, bl) Grant Heilman, (cl) William E. Ferguson, (b) L. L. T. Rhodes/Earth Scenes; **18**(tl, tr) Grant Heilman, (tl, tr, br insets) HBJ, (br) Cary Wolinsky/Stock, Boston; **19**(tl, br), Grant Heilman, (tl, tr, br insets) HBJ, (tr) Cary Wolinsky/Stock, Boston; **20**(both), HBJ; **21**(tl, cr) HBJ, (tr) Robert Sheppard/Frozen Images, (b) Jim Brandenburg/Frozen Images; **22**, HBJ; **24**(tl), Freda Leinwand/Monkmeyer, (tr) E. R. Degginger, (bl, br) Grant Heilman; **25**, Sybil Shelton/Peter Arnold; **26**(all), HBJ;

UNIT 3: 28-29, William H. Calvert/E. R. Degginger, **30**(t), Fritz Prenzel/Bruce Coleman, (bl) George & Judy Manna/Photo Researchers, (cr) Hal H. Harrison/Grant Heilman, (br) Grant Heilman; **31**(tl), E. R. Degginger, (tr) Richard Kolar/Animals Animals, (bl) Tom McHugh/Photo Researchers, (cr) Breck P. Kent/Animals Animals, (br) Stephen Dalton/Animals Animals; **32**(tl), George H. Harrison/Grant Heilman, (tr) Charles Palek/Tom Stack & Assoc., (cl) Gunter Ziesler/Peter Arnold, (bl) Leonard Lee Rue III/Image Bank, (br) W. Perry Conway/Grant Heilman; **34**(t), Jen & Des Bartlett/Bruce Coleman, (b) Grant Heilman; **35**, Zig Leszczynski; **36**(tl), Leonard Lee Rue III/Tom Stack & Assoc., (tr) Malcolm S. Kirk/Peter Arnold, (cr) Oxford Scientific Films/Animals Animals, (b) Hans Rheinhard/Bruce Coleman; **37**(t), Lynn M. Stone/Animals Animals, (bl) Marc N. Boulton/Bruce Coleman, (br) Grant Heilman; **38**(tl), Isidor Jeklin/Animals Animals, (tr) Esao Hashimoto/Animals Animals, (b) Norman Myers/Bruce Coleman; **39**(tl), Warren Garst/Tom Stack & Assoc., (tr) E. R. Degginger, (b) Wildlife Photographers/Bruce Coleman; **40**(tl), Raymond A. Mendez/Animals Animals, (tr, b) E. R. Degginger; **41**, HBJ; **42**(tl), Animals Animals, (tr) David C. Fritts/Animals Animals, (bl) Thomas Houland/Grant Heilman, (br) Grant Heilman;

UNIT 4: 44(l), John Running/Frozen Images, (tr) Richard Hutchings/Photo Researchers, (br) Bob Firth/Frozen Images; **45**(t), HBJ, (bl) B. Kreye/Image Bank, (bc) C. Allan Morgan/Peter Arnold, (br) Joy Glenn Klimek; **46**, E. R. Degginger; **47**(tl) Harry Engels/Animals Animals, (tr) Michael Nabicht/Animals Animals, (b) R. F. Head/Animals Animals; **48**(tl), F. E. Unverhau/Animals Animals, (r) Leonard Lee Rue III/Animals Animals, (bl) Marty Stouffer/Animals Animals; **49**(t), Leonard Lee Rue III/ Animals Animals, (bl) Gary W. Griffin/Animals Animals, (br) Ronald Orenstein/Animals Animals; **50**(tl), Hans Reinhard/Bruce Coleman, (tr) Miriam Austerman/Animals Animals, (b) Helen Williams/Photo Researchers; **51**(t), Hans Reinhard/Bruce Coleman, (b) Russ Kinne/Photo Researchers; **52**(t), Andy Young/Photo Researchers, (bl) Alan G. Nelson/Animals Animals, (br) Zig Leszczynski/Animals Animals; **53**, HBJ; **54**(t), Werner Meinel/Taurus, (c) Scott Ransom/Taurus, (b) Carl Purcell/Photo Researchers;

UNIT 5: 56(l), Peter Southwick/Stock, Boston, (r) Guido Alberto Rossi/Image Bank; **57**(t), E. R. Degginger, (bl) Christiana Dittmann/Rainbow, (br) Grant Heilman; **58**(t), John Serro/Photo Researchers, (b) Bill Noel Kleeman/Tom Stack & Assoc.; **59**, E. R. Degginger; **60**(both), **61**, HBJ; **62**, Grant Heilman; **63**, Bill Gause/Photo Researchers; **64**, Dennis Fisher/International Stock Photos; **65**, Grant Heilman; **66**(tl & bl), Manuel Rodriguez, (br) Thomas Ives; **67**(tl),

(continued on page 168)

Contents

BLUE

HBJ

—Nova ✳ Edition—

SCIENCE

Growing Up Healthy

1

You were small.

2

Now you are bigger.

What can you do now?

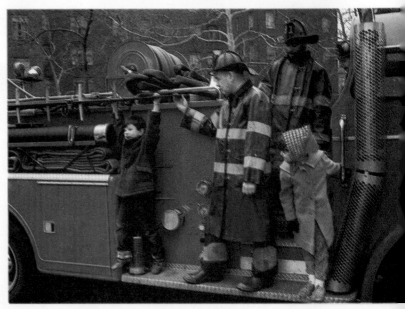

You will grow up.
What can you do then?

Find Out How Tall You Are.

Do this with a friend.

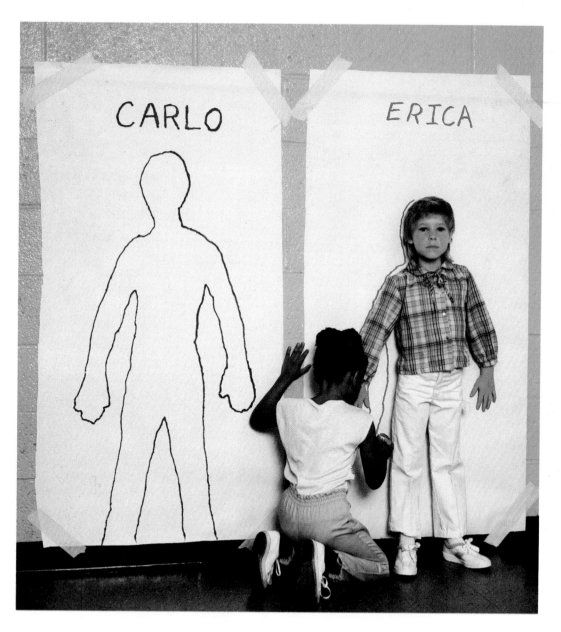

Is everyone the same?

What keeps you healthy?

Food helps you to grow.

What foods are good for you?

Where Does Our Food Come From?

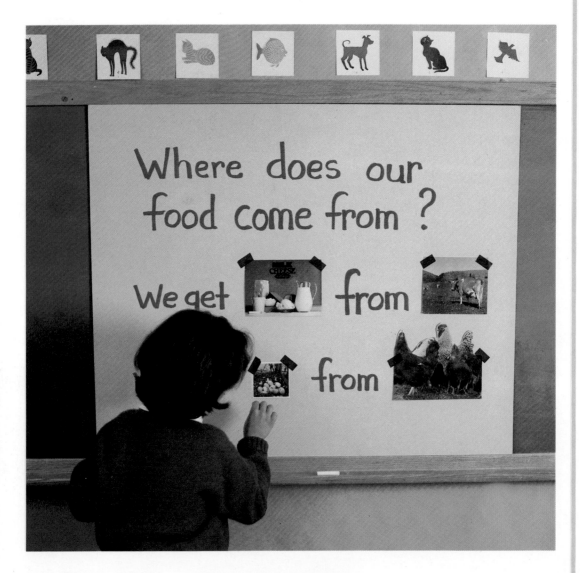

Find or draw pictures of foods.
Find or draw pictures that show
where foods come from.

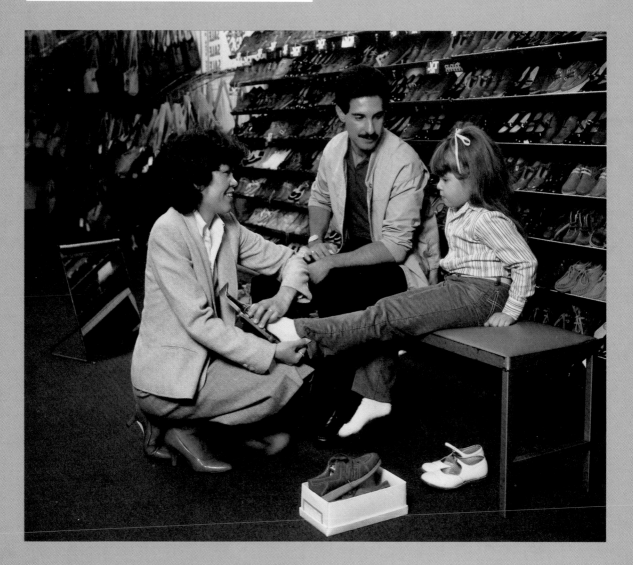

You grow.

Your feet grow, too.

Who helps you get shoes that fit?

You grow and change.

You need to sleep.

You need to play.

You need to eat
good foods.

Which things do you use
when you are bigger?

Which keep you healthy?

More and More Plants

15

There are many kinds of plants.

How are they different?

Many plants grow
from seeds.
A seed grows its own
kind of plant.

What kind of plant will
grow from each seed?

What Do Seeds Need to Grow?

Plant 3 seeds in each cup.

Put water in cup A each day.

Do not put water in cup B.

What happens?

How do plants get water?

What Do Plants Need to Grow?

Put a plant in the light.

Put a plant in the dark.

Water them each day.

What will happen?

This plant gets light.

It gets water.

Is it growing?

This plant gets no light.

It gets water.

Is it growing?

Why?

Plants grow in many places.
Where do you see plants grow?

This man works with plants.

He knows what plants need.

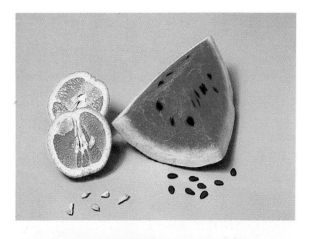

Many plants grow
from seeds.

There are many kinds of
seeds.

Each seed grows its own
kind of plant.

Plants need soil and
water.

Plants need light.

What will grow from each seed?

What do plants need to grow?

More and More Animals

There are many kinds of animals.
How are these animals different?

Tell how these animals
move around.

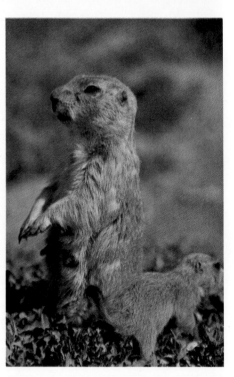

Look at all the young animals.
Many young animals look like
their parents.

Make a Home for This Animal.

Keep it in a warm place.

What happens?

Some animals hatch from eggs.
What animals are hatching?

These animals are mammals.

Mammals do not hatch from eggs.

They are born ready to move.

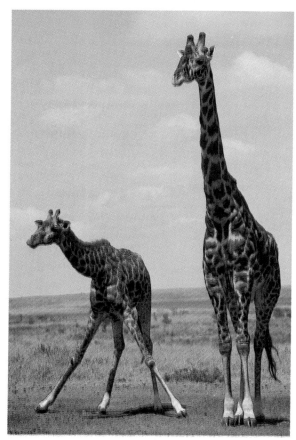

Which of these mammals
do you know?

Some animals take care
of their young.

These young animals get
their own food.

They take care of themselves.

Have you ever seen these animals?

This woman owns the pet store.

What animals would you find there?

Many young animals look like their parents.

Some animals hatch from eggs.

Mammals do not hatch from eggs.

Some animals take care of their young.

42

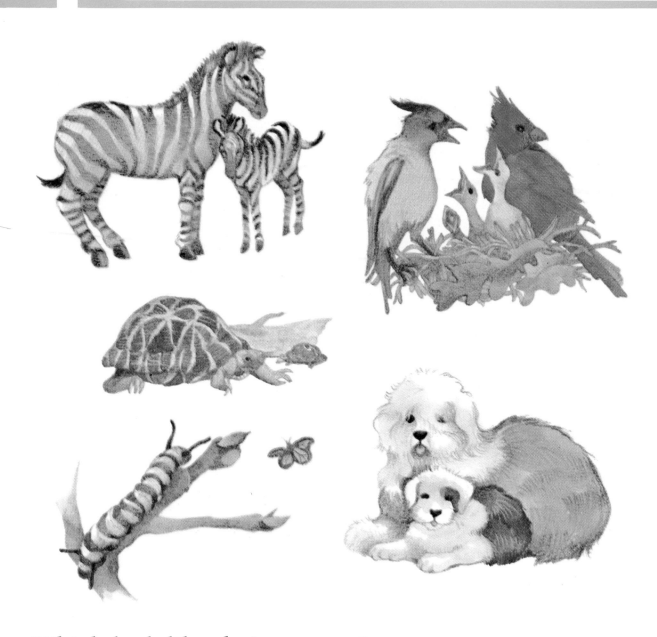

Which look like their parents?

Which hatch from eggs?

Which take care of their young?

Living
and Growing

45

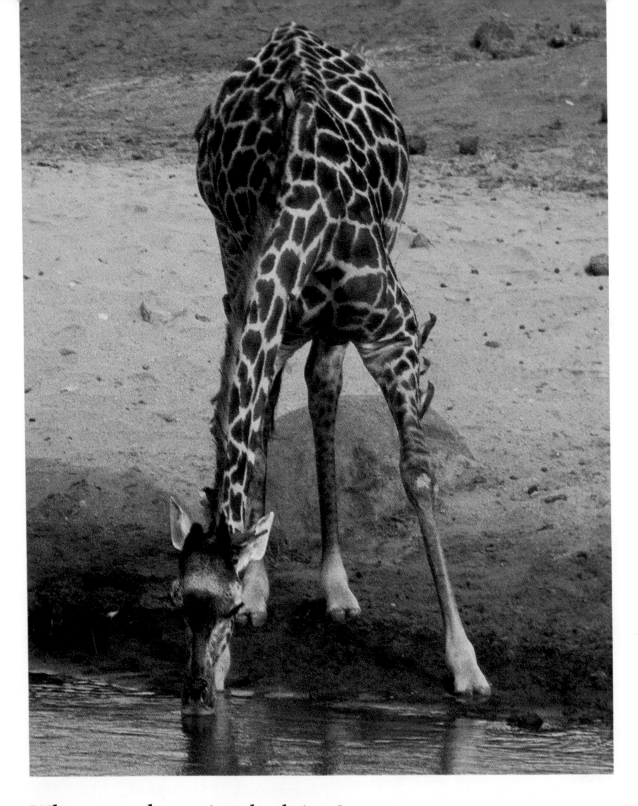

What are the animals doing?

Why?

Animals need food and water.
Animals need a place to live.

Where do these animals live?

Young animals grow as
big as their parents.

Which animal will grow biggest?

Who helps this animal
stay healthy?

Animals need food
and water.

Animals need a
place to live.

Young animals grow as
big as their parents.

Which show what animals need?

Which animal will grow biggest?

Earth, Our Home

The insects eat small plants.

Fish eat the insects.

This animal eats fish.

Animals need food.

Where do they get their food?

Do animals and plants need each other?

Make a Home for Fish.

Put in sand.
Put in water.
Put in small
rocks.

Put in plants.
Put in snails
and fish.

Feed the fish each day.

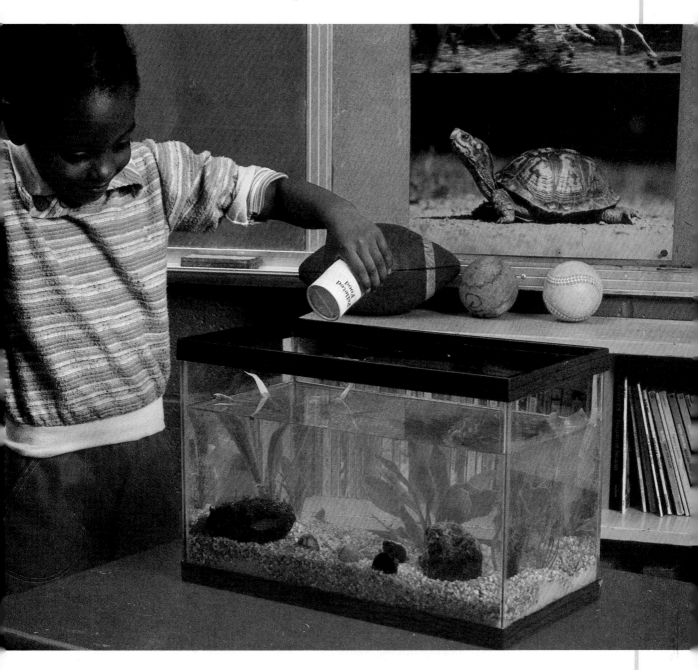

Do animals and plants need each other?

Insects lived here.
So people sprayed around the lake.
The insects died.

Some spray got into the lake.
It made some fish sick.

The owl comes to the lake.

It eats fish.

What might happen to the owl?

We need clean air to live.
We need clean water, too.

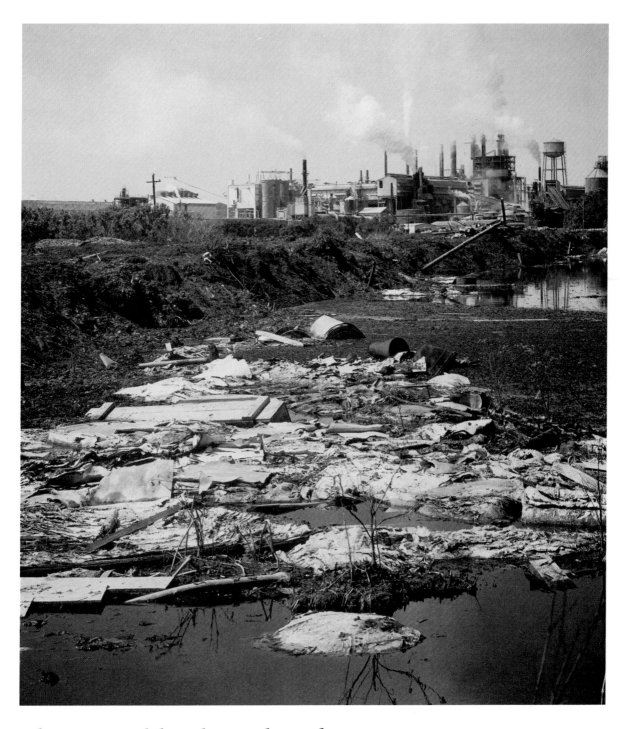

The air and land are dirty here.

The water is dirty, too.

What might happen to people?

There are very few of these plants.
There are very few of these animals.

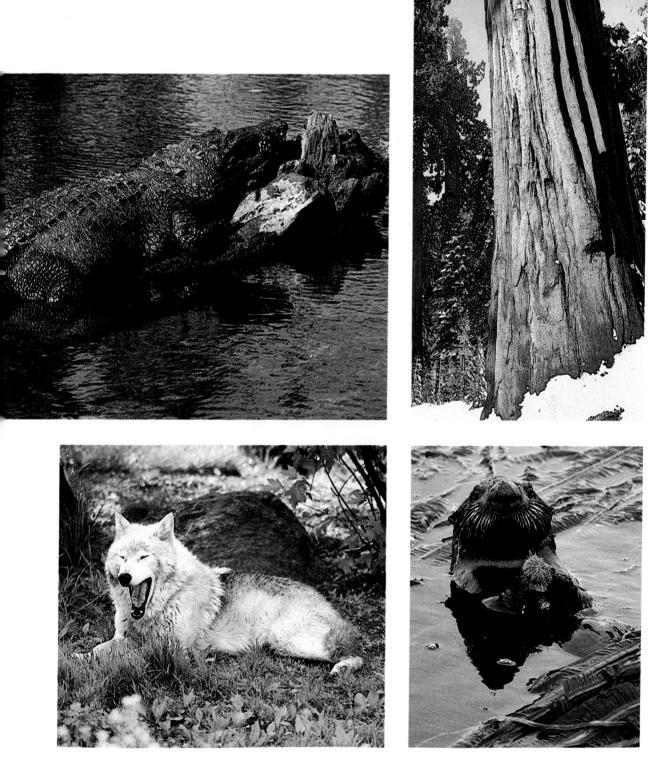

People try to save them.

Earth is home for all living things.

We must take care of the Earth.

How can we help take care of our Earth?

How does he help take
care of our Earth?

Plants and animals need each other.

We need clean air and water.

Dirty water and air can make living things sick.

We must take care of our Earth.

Tell how these animals
get their food.

Find the things that
can make us sick.

What can we do to help?

Matter All Around You

All things are made of matter.
The glass and wood are matter.

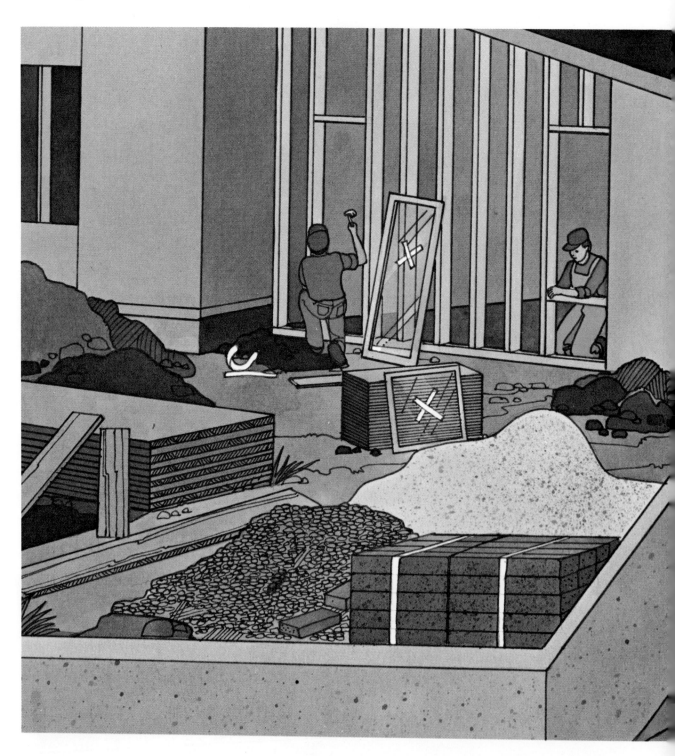

What else is made of matter?

There are three forms of matter.
Solids are one form of matter.
These are solids.

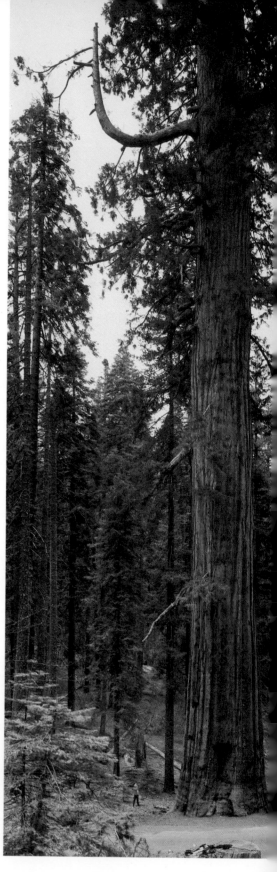

Solids can be small.
Solids can be large.

Solids can be hard.
Solids can be soft.
All solids have a shape.

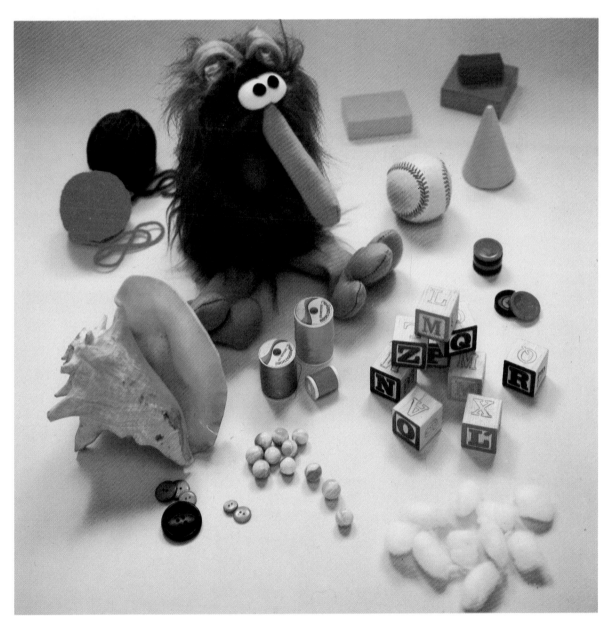

What shapes do you
see here?

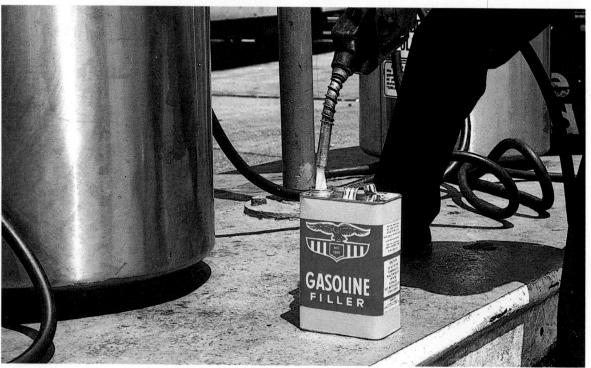

Liquids are another form of matter.

You can pour a liquid.

Do liquids change shape?

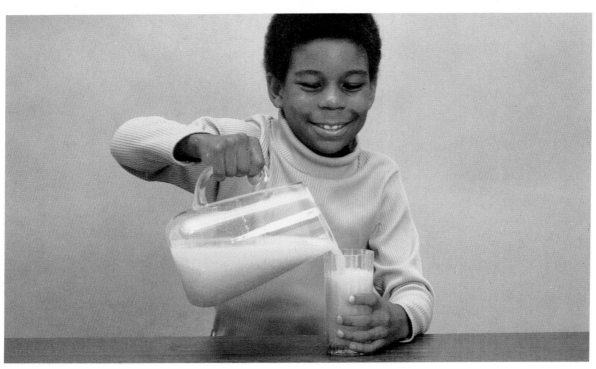

Gases are matter, too.

Air is a gas.

You cannot see air.

Wave your hands fast.

Do you feel air moving?

What is air doing
in each picture?

Is the Glass Empty?

Put a glass in water like this.

Tip the glass slowly.
What comes out of the glass?
What are the bubbles made of?

What matter does a diver use?

All things are made of matter.

There are three
forms of matter.

Solids are one form
of matter.

Liquids are another
form of matter.

Gases are matter, too.

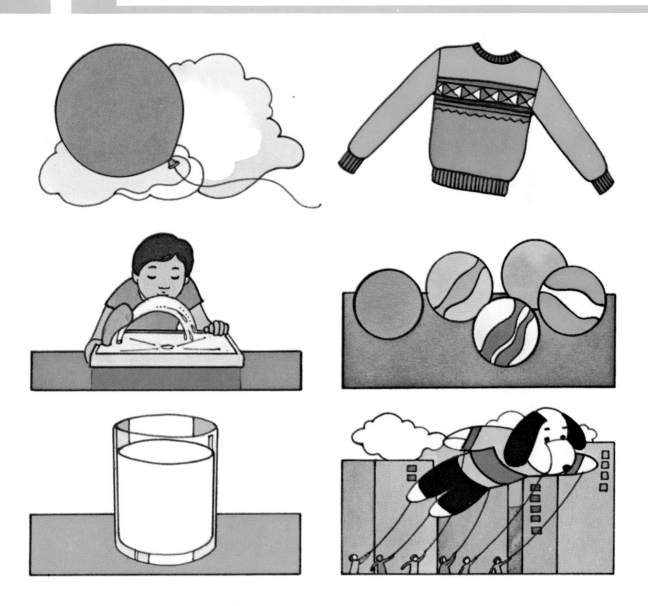

Which are made of matter?

Which are solids?

Which are liquids?

Where are the gases?

Rain or Shine

Some days it rains.

Some days it does not rain.

Does It Rain Where You Live?

Make a chart.

Show the kind of day it is.

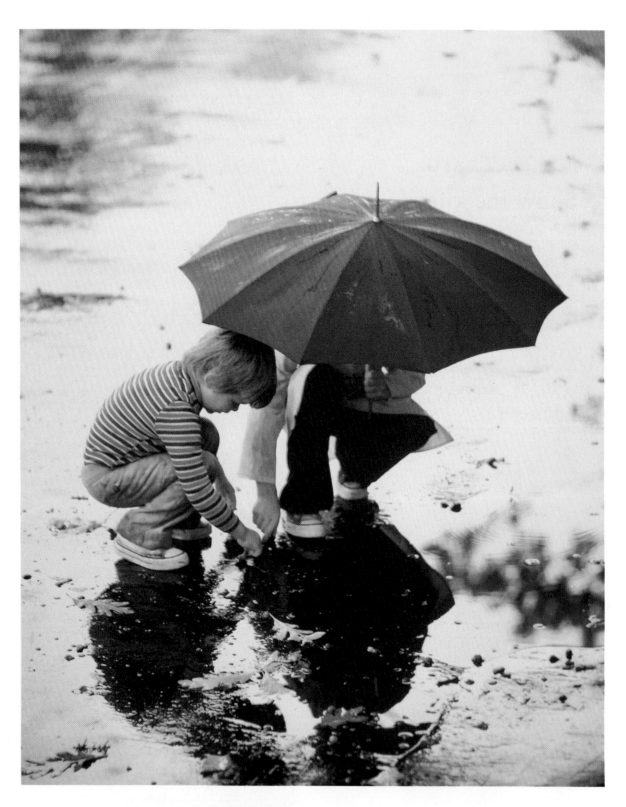

Rain comes from clouds.

Look at the little cloud.
It is made of tiny
drops of water.

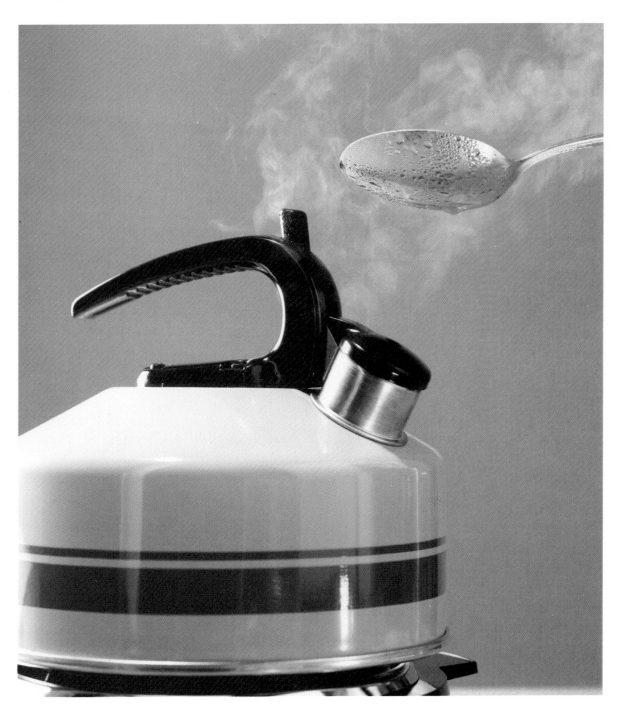

Have you ever seen
clouds like these?

Big clouds are made
of tiny drops of water, too.

Water goes into the air.
Where do clouds get water?

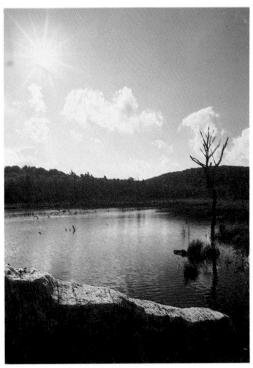

The Sun helps water
go into the air.

Which Will Dry Faster?

Put a little water on each plate.

Which will dry faster?

Who tells you if it will rain?

Some clouds
bring rain.

Clouds are made of
tiny drops of water.

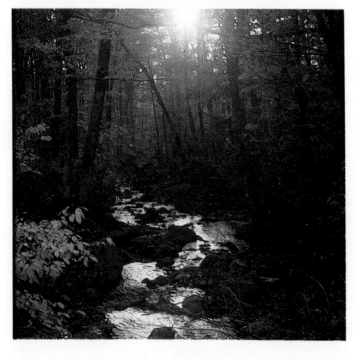

Clouds get water
from many places.

The Sun helps water
go into the air.

Where does rain come from?

What are clouds made of?

Where do clouds get water?

What makes water go into the air?

Day and Night

We get light and heat
from the Sun.

We have day.

Is it always day?

We have night.

Is it always night?

The Sun is lighting part
of the Earth.

Part of the Earth is dark.
That part has night.

Find Out About Day and Night.

Where is it day?

Where is it night?

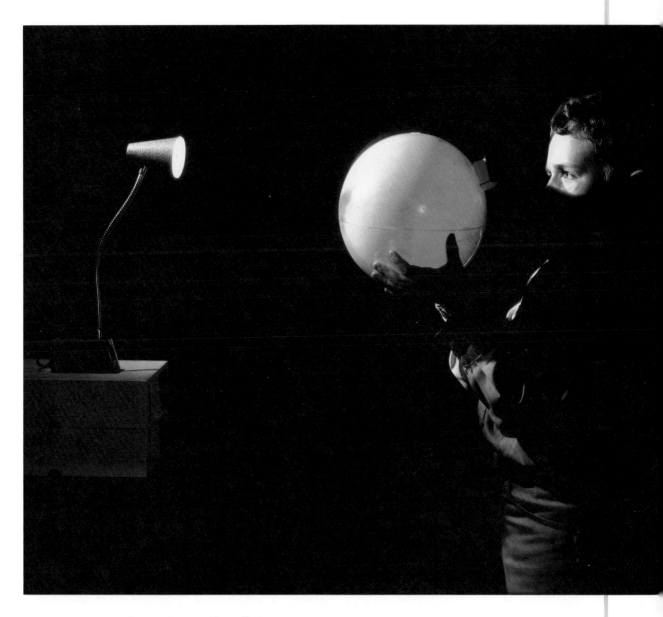

Turn the Earth this way.

Now where is it day?

Where is it night?

Why do we have day and night?

The Earth turns all the time.
Soon it will be dark here.
Why?

Some people work in the day.
Some people work at night.
They keep you safe day and night.

We get light and heat
from the Sun.

We have day and night
because the Earth turns.

Which gives off light and heat?

What happens when the Sun
shines on the Earth?

Push and Pull

113

A push can move something.

A pull can move something.

Which people are pushing?
Which people are pulling?

Which takes more force?

Why?

Which Takes More Force?

Push the book.

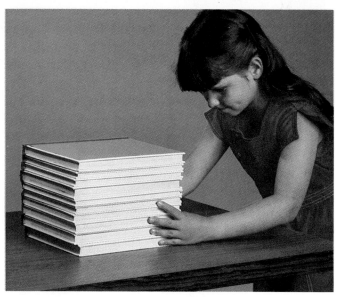

Push the books.

Which takes more force?
Why?

Where is it easier to move?

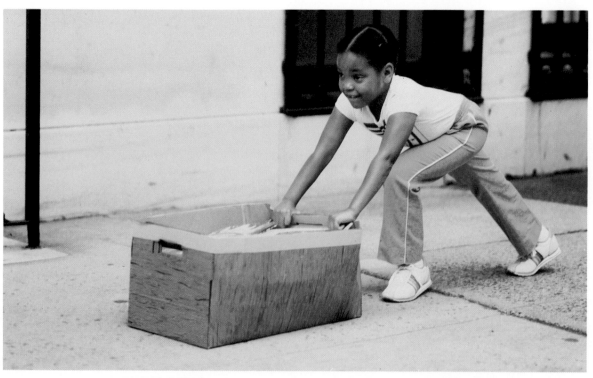

Which Is Easier to Move?

Pull it.

Pull it now.

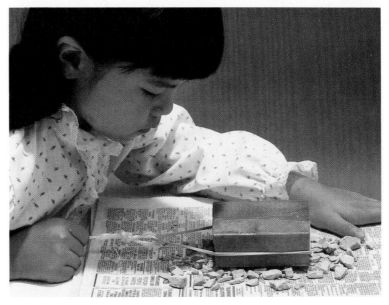

Which is easier to move?
Why?

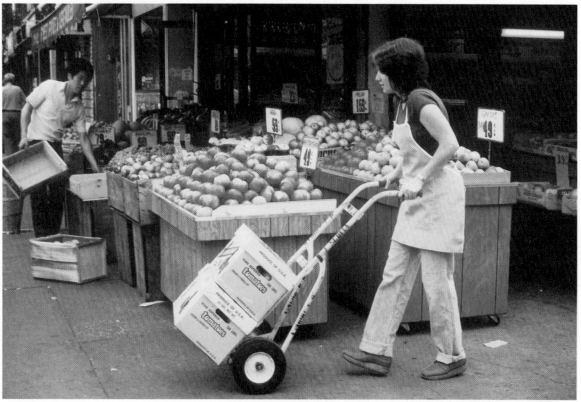

Which way is easier?

Wheels Help Us.

Push the
truck.

Push it
now.

Which is easier?
Why?

We use wheels at work and play.

These people make buildings.

Do they use wheels?

Do they push and pull?

A push or pull can move something.

Heavy things take
more force to move.

It is easy to move
things here.

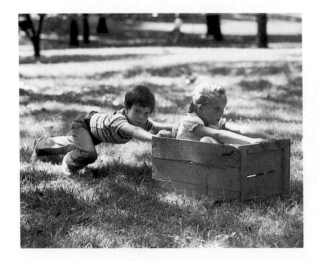

It is not easy to
move things here.

Wheels make things
easier to move.

Which takes more force?

Where is it easier to move?

Which way is easier?

Down and Up

127

What makes them come down?

Gravity pulls them down.

It takes force to lift them.

Which takes more force to lift?

Why?

Which is easier?

Inez goes up the stairs.

Bert goes down the stairs.

Which is easier?

Magnets can lift things.

How do we use magnets?

What Can a Magnet Lift?

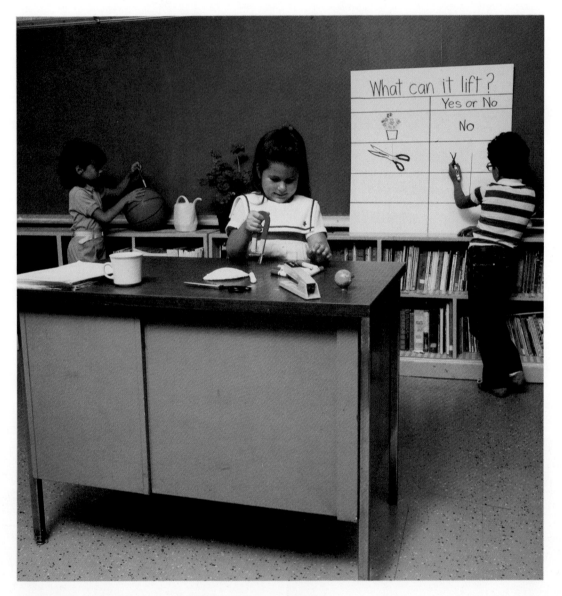

Touch things with a magnet.

What can a magnet lift?

Make a chart to show these things.

The crane has a big magnet.
What does the magnet lift?

Gravity pulls
things down.

It takes force to
lift things.

Heavy things take
more force to lift.

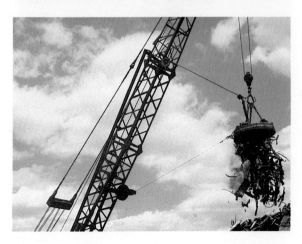

Magnets can lift
some things.

Test Yourself

What makes them come down?

Which takes more force to lift?

Which can a magnet lift?

Earth, Long Ago

139

The Earth was different
long ago.

The plants were different, too.

Dinosaurs lived on the Earth
long, long ago.

Have you ever seen a dinosaur?

The mammoth lived long ago.
It was big and hairy.
Does it look like an
animal you know?

Cave people hunted them
for food and clothing.

The mammoths died out long ago.

The saber-toothed cat
lived long ago.

Does it look like an
animal you know?

How do we know about animals
that lived long ago?

Make a Model Fossil.

Press something in the clay.
Let the clay dry.
Cover the fossil with sand.

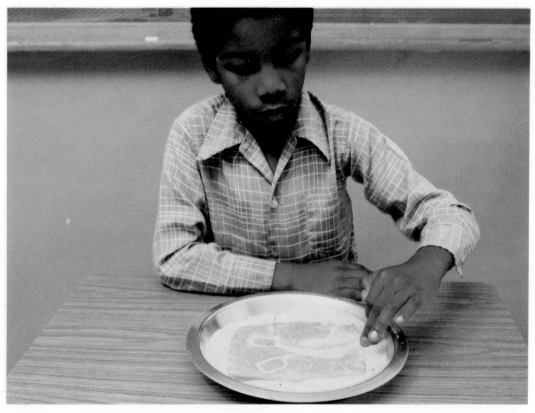

Let a friend find the fossil.
Let a friend guess what it is.

How do we know about
mammoths?

This young mammoth was found
in the frozen ground.

How did it keep so long?

Animals came to tar pools
many years ago.

Some got stuck.
What do you think happened?

People found bones in the tar.
The bones came from an animal.

Can you tell what kind
of animal it was?

How do scientists find out
about animals of long ago?

The Earth was different long ago.

Many animals died out.

We know about these animals from fossils.

What was the Earth like long ago?

Which animals died out?

How do we know about animals
that lived long ago?

Picture Glossary

air

We need *air* to live. **64**

animals

There are many kinds of *animals*. **30**

born

The baby pigs were *born* in May. **36**

clouds

Rain comes from *clouds*. **92**

dark

It is *dark* at night. **22**

day

The Sun is out during the *day*. **103**

dinosaurs

Dinosaurs were big animals. **141**

Earth

Earth is where people live. **68**

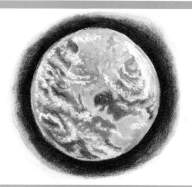

eggs
These animals were hatched from *eggs*.   **34**

food
We eat *food* to help us grow.   **8**

force
It takes *force* to move things.   **116**

fossil
He found a *fossil* in the rocks.   **146**

gases

Gases are one form of matter. **82**

gravity

Gravity pulls things down. **129**

grow

You will *grow* taller. **4**

hatch

Some animals *hatch* from eggs. **34**

healthy
Eating good food can keep
you *healthy*. **6**

heat
The Sun gives us *heat*
and light. **102**

insects
Insects are very small
animals. **58**

land
People live on
land. **65**

lifts

You can *lift* the books. **129**

light

The *light* from the Sun made the plant grow. **22**

liquids

You can pour *liquids*. **80**

living

Plants are *living* things. **68**

magnet

Magnets can lift
things.   **133**

mammals

Mammals are animals with
fur or hair.   **36**

mammoth

The *mammoth* was a big
and hairy animal.   **142**

matter

Matter is what all things
are made of.   **76**

move
Children *move*
as they run.　**31**

night
It is dark at *night*.　**103**

parents
Parents take care of
their young.　**32**

plants
There are many kinds
of *plants*.　**16**

pull

Can you *pull* the
wagon closer?   **114**

push

Can you *push*
the swing?   **114**

rains

The Sun does not come out
when it *rains*.   **90**

saber-toothed cat

The *saber-toothed cat* was a
large animal.   **144**

seeds

Seeds are parts of plants. **18**

soil

Plants need *soil* and water to grow. **26**

solids

Solids are things you cannot pour. **78**

Sun

The *Sun* gives us heat and light. **95**

tar pools
The animals got stuck in
the *tar pools*. **149**

water
Plants need *water*
to live. **21**

wheels
Wheels make things easier
to move. **121**

young
Some animals take care
of their *young*. **38**

Index

air, 64, 65, 72; as a gas, 82, 83; in water, 95, 98, 99

animals, 30, 41, 46, 53, 55, 61, 72, 145, 151; caring for young, 38, 39, 42, 43; died out, 143, 151, 152, 153; getting food, 40, 48, 54, 59, 73; hatching from eggs, 34, 35, 42, 43; in tar pools, 149, 150; making a home, 33, 48, 49, 54; mammals, 36, 37, 42; mammoth, 142, 143; moving, 31; needing plants, 59, 61, 72; parents, 32, 42, 43, 50, 54; ready to move, 36; saber-toothed cat, 144; saving, 66, 67; young, 32, 42, 43, 50, 51, 52, 54

born: animals, 36

clouds, 92, 93, 94, 95, 98, 99

dark: Earth, 105, 108; plants in, 22

day: and night, 103, 106, 107, 110; kind of, 90, 91; people working, 109

dinosaurs, 141

Earth: caring for, 69, 70, 71, 72; day and night, 104, 105, 106, 107, 108, 110, 111;

Grant Heilman, (tr) E. R. Degginger, (bl) Zig Leszczynski/Animals Animals, (br) Stephen J. Krasemann/Photo Researchers; 68(t), Michal Heron, (bl) Manuel Rodriguez, (br) E. R. Degginger; 69(tl), W. K. Almond/Stock, Boston, (tr) HBJ, (b) E. R. Degginger; 70(tl, tr, br), HBJ, (bl) Sybil Shackman/Monkmeyer; 72(t), Manuel Rodriguez, (c) Grant Heilman, (b) HBJ;
UNIT 6: 74(l), Ann Hagen Griffiths/Omni-Photo Communications, (tr) Jack Parsons/Omni-Photo Communications, (br) Michal Heron/Woodfin Camp & Assoc.; 75(t), Wil Blanche/DPI, (c) Phoebe Dunn/DPI, (b) L. L. T. Rhodes/Taurus; 78(l), Ray Solowinski/International Stock Photos, (r) Manley Photo/Shostal; 79, HBJ; 80(tl), Charles E. Schmidt/Taurus, (tr, b) HBJ; 81(both), 82, HBJ; 83(tl), Glyn Cloyd/Taurus, (tr, bl) HBJ, (br) Robert Rattner; 84(both), HBJ; 85, Bob Evans/Peter Arnold; 86(tl, tr, bl), HBJ, (br) Annie Griffiths/Frozen Images;
UNIT 7: 88(l), Steve Wilson/Entheos, (tr) Cliff Moore/Taurus, (br) Tom Tracy/Alpha; 89(t), A-Z Collection/Photo Researchers, (bl) D. Davis/FPG, (br) Stephen J. Krasemann/Photo Researchers; 91, HBJ; 92, Edward Lettau/Peter Arnold; 93, HBJ; 94, Tom Stack & Assoc.; 95(l), Farrell Grehan/Photo Researchers, (tr) Daniel Brody/Stock, Boston, (br) Dana Hyde/Photo Researchers; 97, HBJ/Haynes; 98(t), Stephen J. Krasemann/Peter Arnold, (b) Jerome Wyckoff/Earth Scenes;
UNIT 8: 100, J. Alex Langley/DPI; 101, J. Alex Langley/DPI; 102, William E. Ferguson; 103(both), 106, 107, HBJ; 108, Peter Southwick/Stock, Boston; 109(l), Joshua Tree/Editorial Photocolor Archives, (r) Frederick Lewis; 110(t), George H. Harrison/Grant Heilman, (b) HBJ;
UNIT 9: 112(l), Photo Researchers, (tr) Carter L. Hamilton/DPI, (br) Jack Parsons/Omni-Photo Communications; 113(t), Alec Duncan/Taurus, (c) DPI, (b) Ann Hagen Griffiths/Omni-Photo Communications; 114(both), HBJ; 115(tl, tr, bl), HBJ, (br) Pam Hasegawa/Taurus; 117(both), 118(both), 119(both), 120(both), 121(both), HBJ; 122(tl), HBJ/Joosten, (tr) L. L. T. Rhodes/Taurus, (cr) E. R. Degginger/Earth Scenes, (bl) Lenore Weber/Omni-Photo Communications, (br) Robert A. Isaacs/Photo Researchers; 123, Bill Grimes/Leo de Wys; 124(tl), Michal Heron/Monkmeyer, (tr, bl, br), HBJ;
UNIT 10: 126(l), Ken Biggs/Photo Researchers, (r) Nick Nicholson/Image Bank; 127(t), Jerry Downs/Frozen Images, (bl) Phil Degginger, (br) Jon Yeager/Frozen Images; 128(tl), Mimi Forsyth/Monkmeyer, (r) Frank Siteman/Stock, Boston, (bl) HBJ; 129(both), 131(both), 132, 133(all), 134, HBJ; 135, E. R. Degginger/Earth Scenes; 136(t), Larry Trone/DPI, (c) HBJ, (b) Hugh Rogers/Monkmeyer; 145(tl), C. Allan Morgan/Peter Arnold, (tr) Courtesy, Field Museum of Natural History, Chicago, (b) Tom McHugh/Photo Researchers; 146(both), HBJ; 147, The American Museum of Natural History; 150, Courtesy, The Los Angeles County Museum; 151, Michael Collier/Stock, Boston; 152(b), Courtesy, Field Museum of Natural History, Chicago.

8
9
C 0
D 1
E 2
F 3
G 4
H 5
I 6
J 7